Town and Country New Castle

Pastured near Centreville, a solitary hardwood weathers winter.

Kevin Fleming

text by Nancy E. Lynch • edited by Lori Epstein

ISBN 0-9662423-4-3

Industry dawned early in Wilmington, Delaware's largest city and New Castle County seat (preceding pages). Settled as New Sweden in 1638, Wilmington became one of the mid-Atlantic's most important 19th century industrial sites with the manufacture of black powder on Brandywine Creek. The DuPont Company's evolution to the country's largest chemical and materials conglomerate showered prosperity on the city and opened doors for other businesses. Today, numerous manufacturing and financial institutions broaden Wilmington's busy skyline. Favorable incorporation laws attract nearly 60 percent of Fortune 500 companies and Delaware has more Ph.D.s per capita than any other state.

New Jersey shore to port, a waterman (left) checks his crab pots at sunrise on the Delaware River in southern New Castle County. "You can't take your pots out and let them sit — you have to tend them every 72 hours by law," explains commercial crabber Steve Pyle of Odessa. Territorial rights are up for grabs. "It's first come, first served. If you go out and no one's there, you can start laying your lines. Basically, everyone tries to get along," he says of the state's 200 or so licensed crabbers. "You work sunup to sundown, seven days a week but once you've done it you can't give it up."

"I saw this barn and had to have it," Sal De Paulo says of the 19th century stucco, fieldstone and frame outbuilding mirrored in Maple Brook Farm's spring-fed pond near Centreville (following pages). "It was in pretty bad shape when we bought it in 1985. We nailed siding and put a new cedar shake roof on it. Amish from Pennsylvania paint it every five years. Everybody likes it." De Paulo decorates his much-photographed barn on the Kennett Pike with a 14-foot diameter wreath at Christmas and a 20-by-40-foot American flag on Independence Day. The pegged-beam barn is dated 1844 and signed by Benjamin Walker Recktor and John Barton Clark, who inscribed "Learn of me, be humble in these latter days" on its north interior wall. "I'd heard about this barn before we bought it," adds De Paulo's wife, Gerrie. "People take pictures constantly. I'm barned to death."

Serendipity rains on Aaron E. Honie (preceding pages) of Wilmington, son Aaron T. and friend Leondrei Salters-Simmins as they relax in Brandywine Creek. "Actually, there are two waterfalls. To get to this one, you have to use Shaky Bridge which used to be really shaky until they tightened it up," says Honie, an assembly line supervisor at Daimler-Chrysler in Newark. "I live a couple of blocks away on West Street and try to get here every day." Honie swims and fishes above the waterfall, walks his three dogs, bikes and picnics in the park near Brandywine Zoo and Monkey Hill. "I just moved back from Philadelphia and purposely moved to this area. It's relaxing."

"I'm taking advantage of a few minutes prior to a train arrival," explains veteran Amtrak commuter and 25-year employee Ernest E. Chance (right) as he gets some laptop time in Wilmington's 1907 train station. "In fact, I'm working on a memo in regard to high-speed rail operations." A subject Chance, Amtrak's assistant chief mechanical officer in charge of high-speed rail mechanical maintenance, knows well. He's in the thick of Acela, Amtrak's new service. "The name was created from two words, 'accelerate' and 'excellence,' and is the rebranding of Amtrak service in the Northeast Corridor from Washington, D.C. to Boston." Improvements for the millennium include high-speed – 150 miles per hour – rail service for business passengers, regional service up to 125 miles per hour and faster commuter service between Philadelphia and New York. Although Wilmington, Amtrak's fifth busiest station with 700,000 passengers annually, gains platform improvements and passenger amenities, the trackside waiting room's old red oak benches and marble floors remain hallmarks of another era. The last refurbishing was in the mid-1980s for the station listed on the National Register of Historic Places.

"Nobody really wants to be a longshoreman today," says John Uryc (right), a 30-year Port of Wilmington worker. "Most of us load and unload cargo. It's not like building a rocket ship but it's labor-intensive and every week's different. You might make $2,000 one week then, shucks, $100 the next." The Wilmington native reports daily to the International Longshoreman's Association on South Claymont Street. "We're subcontracted out and paid union scale. As long as we work 1,000 hours a year to keep our benefits, there's no squawk." Cargo can be memorable. "We unloaded a ship of eggs from Israel. There was a little star on each one. They were so delicate to work with. Then there was a ship full of onions. That was a doggone stinking job." But the second-generation longshoreman seldom complains. "The freedom of coming to work or not coming to work is the good part. If the big fish are running, I might just go fishing that day."

Gridlock of great import, foreign-made cars line the Port of Wilmington (following pages) which posted its busiest year in 1998 with a record 4.8 million tons of cargo. Imported automobiles jump-started the increase by doubling to 113,366 units while exports by Ford and General Motors rose 25 percent. The port, established in 1923, is recognized as the East Coast gateway for worldwide fruit and produce imports. And more imported bananas and apple, pear and orange juice concentrates flow through Wilmington's docks than any others nationally. The facility also maintains the country's largest on-dock cold storage. Owned and operated by state-owned Diamond State Port Corporation, the port is vital to Wilmington's economy, employing 4,200 workers and paying $14 million in state and local taxes. With a single 4,000-foot pier on the Christina River, the port plans ambitious expansion along the Delaware River.

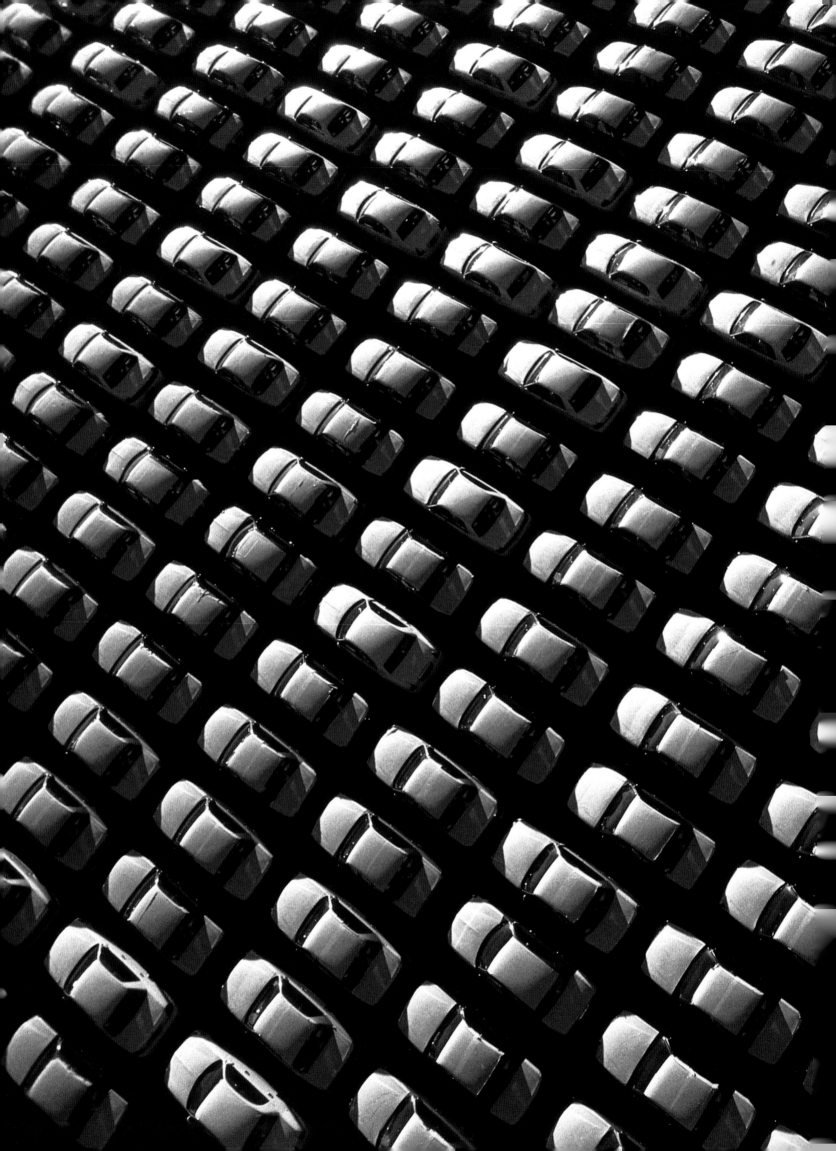

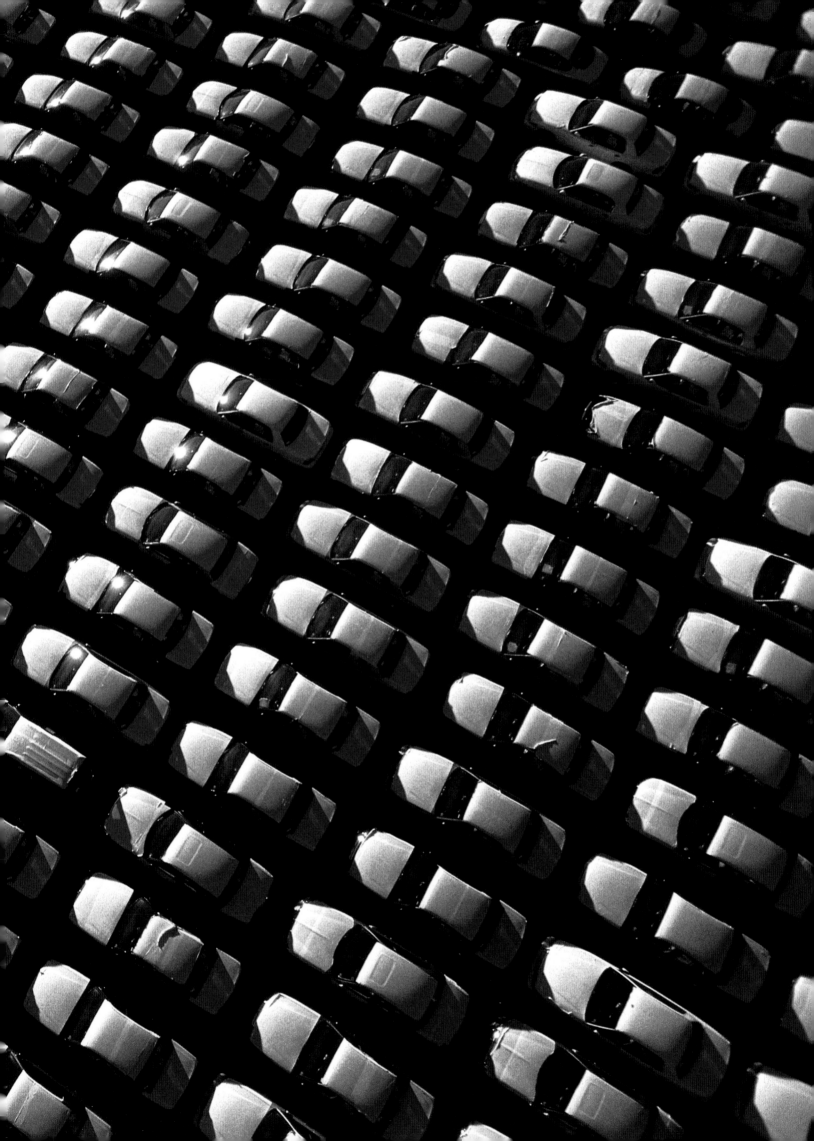

Out of this world, the Saturn L-Series (preceding pages) sends car buyers into orbit. "It's brand stinking new. People have been waiting for this car and the response has been awesome," Saturn Corporation spokeswoman Alice Petitt says. The midsize vehicle, an alternative to the smaller S-Series Saturn, is made only at the company's Wilmington Assembly Plant on Boxwood Road. Retailers debuted the car nationally in July after the corporation, a General Motors subsidiary, invested $1.2 billion and three years of planning to double its Saturn lineup. Annual L-Series production at Wilmington's 2,300-worker plant is expected to tally 200,000 cars on two shifts. "Saturn Corporation has a very loyal customer base. We've interfaced with some of them and it's infectious. It's like an epidemic," says Petitt. "Customers feel a sense of belonging when they own a Saturn product."

Old cars, like this 1934 chopped top three-window Ford Coupe, start Jim Tartaglia's engine (right). "I have a friend, Earl Dunmon, an old-time motorhead, who took me to the Car Cruise near Bear where everyone gets together in all different models. It was a great day." The monthly rally, which geared up years ago, attracts truckloads of vintage car enthusiasts to Fox Run Shopping Center. "I wanted to see what kind of work was done on the frames," recalls Tartaglia, a stone engraver and sandblaster whose restoration credits include a 1918 International huckster and a 1924 GMC oil delivery truck.

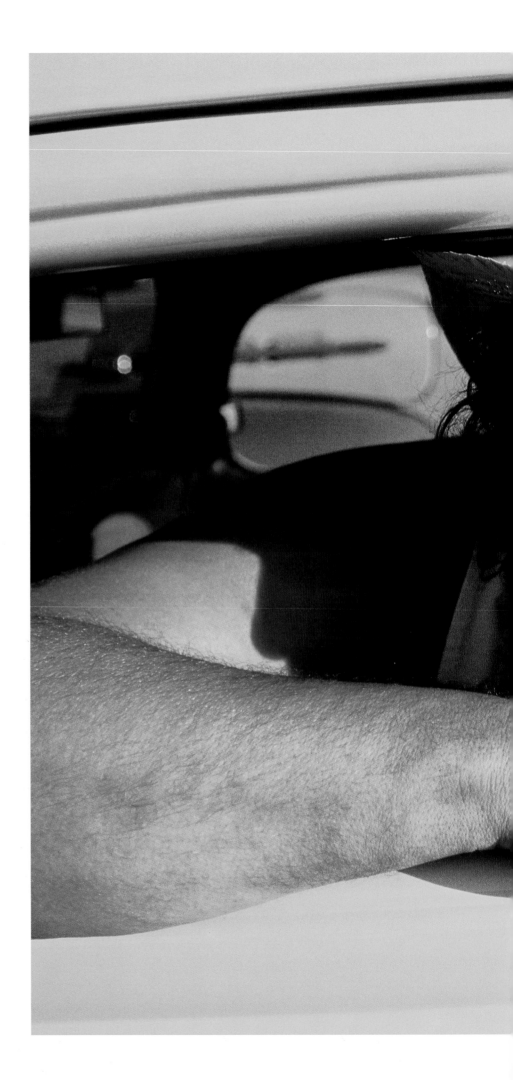

"Wilmington's a great city. It's growing and there are a lot of advantages to living here that encourage families to get together," says lifelong resident Melissa Ewell. Summer in the city means outdoor fun for Fourth Street resident Ikea Dickerson (preceding pages). "I like to jump around and sometimes I practice jump roping," the E.G. Shortlidge Elementary School second-grader says as her mother, Letitia, and brother, Kendell, work the rope for her. "I like it when the sun's coming out so I can be outside and play with my friends."

Having a ball, Dan Johnson swings into action while twin brother Reid plots his next move and neighbor Casey Englebert readies for the rebound (right). "That ball's the best investment I ever made in summer entertainment. My kids play with it every day," the twin's mom, Kim Johnson, says of the oversized vinyl orb in the family's Delaware Avenue backyard. "They kick it, they jump on it. Kids in the neighborhood love it. So do their parents, as long as I keep it in my yard. My husband thought I was crazy because I spent about $100 on this ball. I told him the kids were going to love it. I was right."

"The Blue Danube Ball is the best-kept secret in Delaware," Ruth Babiy says of the elegant fund-raiser in the Hotel du Pont's Gold Ballroom (right) where about 200 gather annually to enjoy Austrian culture. Sumptuous Viennese fare precedes artistic interludes and traditional dances at the black-tie affair sponsored by the Austrian-American Society of Delaware. "You don't have to know how to dance the Polonaise. Everybody takes a partner and it's basically a three-step. Everyone loves to do it," says Babiy, perennial co-chair of the event organized in 1969 by former WDEL radio personality Charlotte Shedd and Adele Weaver.

   Corps de ballet members from the Wilmington Ballet Company (following pages), the city's first resident professional ballet company, fidget in the hotel's marble foyer awaiting their cue to perform. Under the direction of Victor Wesley, ballerinas dance to music in keeping with the ball's Austrian theme. The evening's proceeds provide a $7,000 scholarship to a promising young Delaware musician or singer, chosen through audition at the Wilmington Music School, for six weeks of summer study at the Mozarteum in Salzburg, Austria. New Castle-born Kathleen Cassello, one of the Three Sopranos, earned the 1984 stipend. Each scholarship winner must perform at the Blue Danube Ball "so those attending," Babiy says, "can see what they're sponsoring."

Grand finale, the Russian Ballet Theater of Delaware (preceding pages) bowed out after five years. A projected funding dip forced the professional troupe to stage its final performance at Wilmington's Grand Opera House. Founded in 1994 by dance enthusiast Marsha Borin, the Ballet Theater provided an opportunity for 10 members of a Ukrainian ballet troupe stranded after a 1993 performance in Philadelphia. Although the troupe did well at the box office and was booked through 2001, more than half its budget relied on grants and contributions. "It was the saddest experience I've ever lived through," says Borin, who left her law practice to direct the ballet. "We brought world-class dance to a community that ordinarily would not have had this quality of entertainment. We were just emerging as a company of national repute. It didn't have to end. All the dancers have remained here and we hope one day soon the Russian Ballet will be back on Delaware stages."

Highly visible volunteers Lisa Osberg of Wilmington and Adrianne Spiegleman of Smyrna (right) warm up backstage for Mozart's "Don Giovanni" at Wilmington's Grand Opera House. Mezzo-soprano Andrea Arena (above) of Wilmington, a professional opera singer for three years, exercises her lungs before the performance. "They're 'supers' or supernumeraries which means they do pantomime bits," says OperaDelaware's general director Leland P. Kimball III. He lauds amateurs' active roles in the 55-year-old regional professional opera company, noted for its innovative programming.

Centerpiece of Chateau Country, Granogue (preceding pages) dominates northern New Castle County's rolling hills as a weatherproof reminder of the influence and frequent indulgence of the duPont family in Delaware. Built of Germantown granite over 18 months and completed in 1923 by Irénée duPont, president of the DuPont Company from 1919 to 1926, the 11-bedroom mansion is 362 feet above sea level. Granogue was home to duPont, his wife, Irene, and their eight daughters and a son. For nearly 30 years, it served as backdrop for duPont's lavish Fourth of July fireworks parties. "The structure itself will stand the ages," says current resident Irénée duPont Jr. "It's going to be the devil's own job to tear it down but not on my watch. I look at it as a tool for carrying on the thoughts and philosophy from one generation to another. I have the highest esteem for my parents for giving me that privilege."

A water tower, also of Germantown granite, (right) stands sentry on the 515-acre estate.

Turf's up for thoroughbred and Arabian racing April through October at Delaware Park in Stanton (following pages). Designed by William duPont Jr. and opened in 1937 as the East Coast's only major track outside Aqueduct for June racing, the verdant 600-acre venue hosts the $500,000 Delaware Handicap each July. "We have a reputation for being one of the prettiest tracks around. Our paddock and grove are signature pieces," says Delaware Park spokesman Chris Sobocinski. Leading jockey Mike Smith recently raced at Delaware Park for the first time. "There's a lot of history here. There's also a family atmosphere. You just walk in and see the beautiful saddling area, the big ol' trees. It reminds me a bit of Saratoga." When bettors tire of horses at Delaware's only thoroughbred track, they wager at nearly 2,000 slot machines nearby. "The addition of slots in 1995 allows Delaware Park to increase purses," says Sobocinski. "That makes our product more attractive and lets us stay competitive, now that Baltimore and Pennsylvania have their own tracks."

Conquering hurdles, Winterthur's annual Point-to-Point amateur steeplechase races (right) clear an elitist image with pony rides, dog high-jumping, canine costume competition and kite making. "The event started out in 1979 as really something for horse people but it's grown to be so much more," says Hillary K. Holland of Winterthur. The tailgate picnic contest, pony races (above) and antique carriage parade remain staples. The one-day May fundraiser attracts crowds of 26,000 and has netted more than $3.3 million for Henry Francis duPont's acclaimed early American decorative arts museum and gardens north of Wilmington.

An armillary sphere, an astronomical instrument that shows positions of important circles of the celestial sphere, is the focal point of Winterthur's Sundial Garden (following pages). "We've got something for everyone with rooms, galleries, gardens and a research library," Holland says. "And we're open 362 days a year so we can certainly keep you occupied."

Even with 175 period rooms, Winterthur always dresses for the holidays, re-creating seasonal celebrations of the 18th and 19th centuries. The duPont Dining Room (left) and Montmorenci Staircase (above) deck the halls, bringing to life Lucy Ellen Merrill's circa 1870 drawing, "A Victorian Dining Room at Christmas," with Yuletide greens and stacks of presents at each place. By adding a second flight to a circa 1822 circular staircase from North Carolina, duPont, who died in 1969, created an unusual elliptical shape.

Pretty as a picture, Laura Jogani (right) of Corner Ketch embraces her unusual family tree. "She and her younger sister, Elizabeth, are 50 percent Polish and 50 percent Indian," Suken Jogani says of his progeny. "My wife, Maria, is 100 percent Polish and I'm 100 percent Indian. Chances are they might be the only Polish-Indian kids in the state. It's not a very common mix." The couple met at the DuPont Company's Ag Products Division and recently returned to their Wilmington roots after a transfer to East Peoria, Illinois. "We're close to family, the neighborhood has lots of kids and we like the rolling hills," says Jogani. "We like the ruralness of it even though it's not really rural."

"This is one of the few private residences in the state that gets a comment from historian J. Thomas Scharf which tickles the hell out of me," Fritz Haase says of his 1877 Middletown home (preceding pages). In Scharf's ***History of Delaware***, the First State's foremost chronicler describes the North Cass Street house of his friend and then-governor Benjamin Thomas Biggs as "a handsome residence." "It's the Addams family look," quips Haase. The partially restored Second Empire Mansard-style structure receives its annual floral flourish from his wife, Donna, and neighbor Laszlo Bodo. "The etched flash glass on both sides of the front double door with faux graining is absolutely fabulous," Donna says. Biggs died in the house on Christmas Day, 1893. "We've heard lots of tiny footsteps. It doesn't feel like a haunted house and it isn't scary, but you can feel a presence."

Lost in his field of dreams, Tyler Warrington (following pages) of Hockessin watches a Delaware Semi-Pro League baseball game at Rockford Park. "He's a baseball fanatic. He eats, sleeps and drinks the game," says dad Alan, a Pike Creek family physician and head coach of HealthSouth, one of eight Delaware Semi-Pro teams. "Some nights he's a batboy and other nights he's just a big fan. He always likes to have a catch with the players."

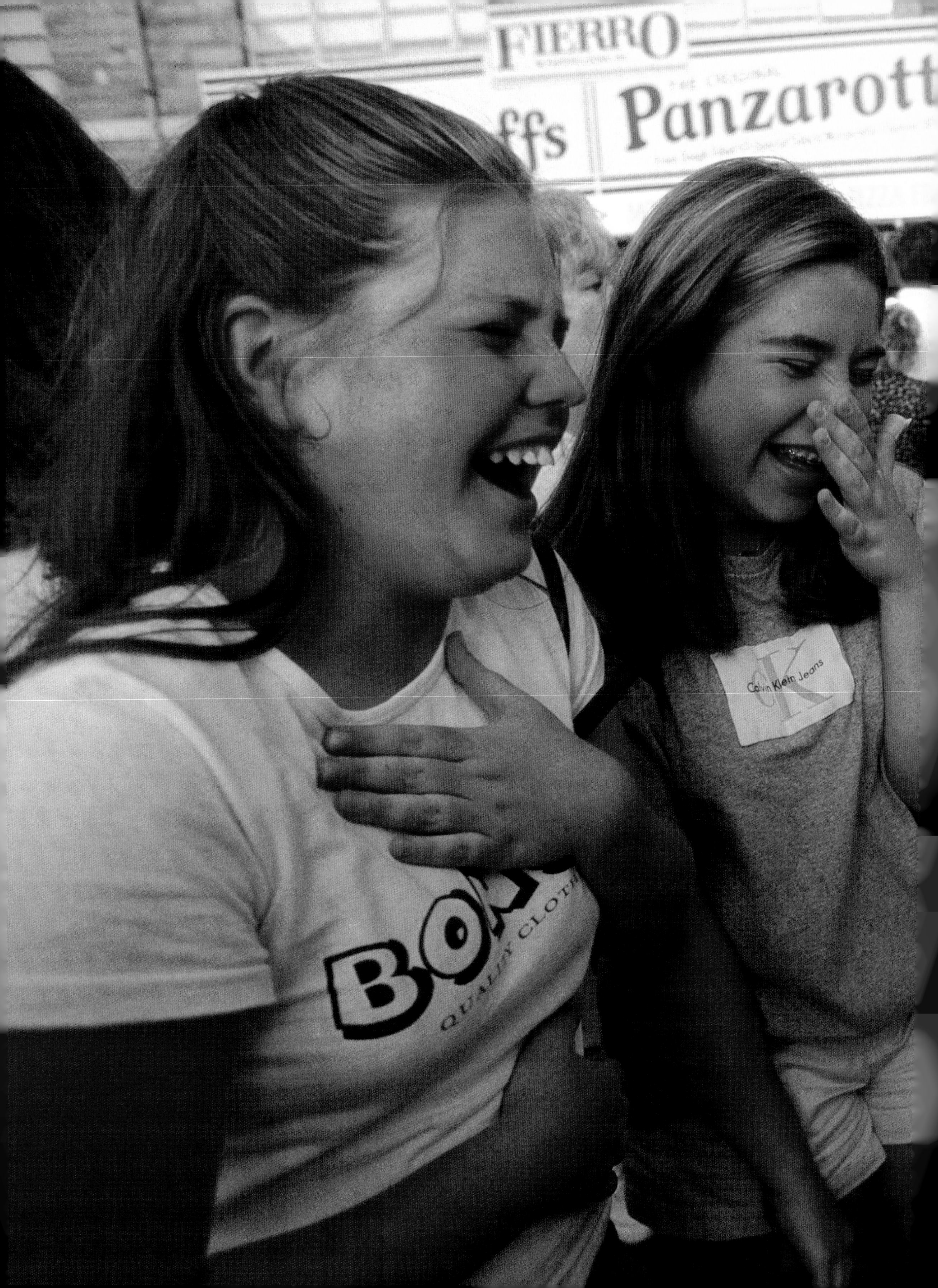
FIERRO
Panzarott
Calvin Klein Jeans

Entertainment arcs over St. Anthony of Padua Roman Catholic Church (left) during the Italian Festival, Wilmington's first major ethnic celebration. Italians flocked to the city in the 1880s as construction workers for the Baltimore and Ohio Railroad, living in boxcars before clustering in row houses on Wilmington's west side. Community spirit galvanized Little Italy in the 1920s when the Roman Catholic diocese created an Italian parish. St. Anthony's Church dominates the neighborhood in size and spirit.

The June festival, organized in 1975 to celebrate the church's 50th anniversary, musters 600 volunteers and attracts 250,000 people who spend $1 million on food, rides, games and entertainment. Proceeds benefit church programs and St. Anthony's schools. "It's a really big festival. I like the rides best. The Zipper's so scary it's a lot of fun. I've been going since I was little and always meet my friends there," says Meghan Procak (preceding pages).

The festival's final component, marked by a homing pigeon release (above) on the eighth day, is an hourlong procession through Little Italy to celebrate the feast of St. Anthony, the parish's patron saint who fed the poor. Carried on a float, the larger-than-life statue (following pages) symbolically oversees distribution of thousands of rolls along the route. "Our celebration pulls people together," says Phil Durnan, chair with Joan Dearie and Anthony Lano. "It's an upbeat event and everybody comes back year after year. That's the greatest part of the whole thing."

Fun comes in all flavors for Jenny Neuwien (right) as she nibbles on Joseph Sands at St. Hedwig's 43rd Polish Festival in Wilmington. "We were just having a good time," says Neuwien, whose family reunites at the city's oldest festival. "My dad, Nicky Neuwien, is a member of the church and he calls us every year. About 12 of us get together. It's nice to see everyone." The six-day festival's Polish food and polka bands always prove good habits for Felician Sisters Dorothy and Angela of Sacred Heart Convent. "It was the first time I'd been on a ride like that for 30 years," Sister Dorothy says of the Sizzler. "And it'll probably be another 30 years."

Completed in 1859 with granite walls up to 30 feet thick and massive firepower to protect the ports of Wilmington and Philadelphia, Fort Delaware on Pea Patch Island (preceding pages) in the Delaware River was the nation's largest and most advanced military fortification. Indoor flush toilets provided novel relief at the fort, constructed over 10 years at a cost of $2 million. During the Civil War, the pentagon-shaped Union fortress was converted to a prisoner-of-war camp and incarcerated nearly 13,000 Confederates after the Battle of Gettysburg. Such concentrations of troops and prisoners made the 70-acre island community east of Delaware City the state's most populous during this era. Many of the 2,700 prisoners who died here were buried in a national cemetery across the river at Finn's Point, New Jersey. The fort, unique for its circular granite stairways and 30-foot moat, also was garrisoned during the Spanish-American War and both World Wars. No hostile shots ever were fired from Fort Delaware. Closed in 1944, the fortress was declared surplus federal property. Delaware acquired it three years later and turned it into one of its first state parks.

Accessible only by boat, Fort Delaware draws big numbers for Garrison Weekend every August. "It's our premier event. We bring in 300 interpreters from all over the East Coast to show what life was like in 1864," spokeswoman Elaine Derrickson says of the cooks, blacksmiths, laundresses, sutlers, soldiers, politicians and prisoners like John Clarkson (right) of Shipman, Virginia who bring history to life. The Fort Delaware Society, organized in 1950, advises the state on the fort's preservation and interpretation and maintains the museum, library, archives and gift shop.

Union re-enactors ponder battlefield strategy over coffee at Brandywine Creek State Park (preceding pages) where Civil War engagements are waged every Memorial Day weekend. "Battles start at 1 p.m. and last 45 minutes to an hour. Yanks win one and Confederates win one," seasonal park employee Jonathan Schneider says of the 1,500 East Coast re-enactors who occupy the park's 1,000 acres. "We're the only Delaware state park that does re-enacting. We have stone walls and open fields and even though no Civil War battles were ever fought here, it looks conceivable." Nearly 10,000 spectators pay $15 a vehicle for campsite tours, artillery demonstrations and period fashion shows before the war begins. Proceeds support Fort Delaware. "The re-enactors fight different battles each year in chronological order and make them as authentic as possible. There's something about them that transcends time."

Taking time for summer fun, Jenilee Delvalle (right) and her sister, Nidhya, of Wilmington relax with relatives on a Sunday afternoon near Smith's Bridge on the Brandywine River. "It's a place where we can all be together as a family and have fun," says Jenilee, an Alexis I. duPont High School ninth-grader.

River for all seasons, the rapid-flowing, rock-filled
Brandywine (preceding pages) for centuries
powered sawmills, grist, cotton, woolen, and paper
mills as well as black powder manufacture along
its banks. Early Lenni-Lenape inhabitants called
the waterway Wawaset, meaning "near the bend."
The Brandywine likely derives its name from
Andren Brantwyn, one of Wilmington's first
Swedish settlers.

 The creek, with headwaters in two branches that
converge in Pennsylvania, flows more than 10
miles through northern New Castle County. It falls
eight feet from the state line to Rockland Bridge –
three-quarters of its length – then plummets 130
feet to its confluence with the Christina River.
Now a recreational venue, the Brandywine
supports canoeing, kayaking, tubing, rope-
swinging, swimming, wading and hot weather
cool-downs (right).

The first duPont family home, Eleutherian Mills (preceding pages) immortalizes an immigrant's success. French chemist and political refugee Eleuthère Irénée duPont in 1802 capitalized on water power from Brandywine Creek north of Wilmington to forge the nation's biggest gunpowder business. E.I. Du Pont de Nemours and Company supplied 40 percent of explosives used by Allied Forces during World War I and manufactured black powder at the original Hagley Mills until 1921. Subsequent diversification produced nylon, Dacron, Teflon, Lucite, Lycra and Kevlar, revolutionary inventions that propelled Du Pont to the industrial forefront as the country's largest chemical company. duPont's 1803 manse, on a hill overlooking the mills and home to five generations of duPonts, today is the centerpiece of the restored industrial community known as Hagley Museum. The Georgian-style residence is furnished with antiques and family keepsakes. "It's always decorated at Christmas," says longtime Hagley volunteer Dick Scott, adding that downstairs mantels receive special treatment (left). "What impresses people about the house is it's not ostentatious, it's not showy. It's just a plain, livable house. Visitors expect to see something big and elaborate and it's not." The powder yard contains massive stone mills, storehouses and a waterwheel while Blacksmith Hill focuses on the social and family history of the mill workers.

"Growing poinsettias is a pain in the butt," says Michael Leubecker, manager of Floral Plant Growers near Middletown. "They're a long crop and they take a lot of effort." With greenhouses covering 10 acres, the business wholesales about 500,000 of the showy holiday flowers yearly to mass merchandisers primarily in Delaware, Maryland and Virginia. Worker Kaorn Caim (following pages) from Cambodia carries ready-for-market plants through a sea of Freedom Red poinsettias. "When you look at acres of red, white and pink, they are pretty," Leubecker allows. "But they're prettier when they're in someone's home and paid for."

73

Christmas in Odessa greets thousands each December for day and candlelight tours of 18th and 19th century homes along Appoquinimink Creek. Established in 1964 by the Women's Club of Odessa, the event funds scholarships for area high school graduates and local civic projects. "The appeal," says tour chairman Jeanne L. Hatton, "is the way residents go all out decorating. Their homes are so warm and welcoming." A 19th century card table (left) in the front parlor at The Cottage, the late 1700s log and frame home of William Allen and Margaret Chandler Derrickson, is set for Christmas Eve whist and brandy. At the nearby brick Corbit-Kabis House, an antique silver service (above) reflects season's greetings. Originally Cantwell's Bridge and a bustling grain shipping port, today Odessa is an architectural treasure trove.

Dinner for 10 was always lavish at Rockwood, the north Wilmington estate of merchant banker Joseph Shipley. The Victorian manor house exemplifies mid-19th century Rural Gothic architecture, rare in Delaware. Now a museum owned and operated by New Castle County, Rockwood exhibits English, Continental and American decorative arts. Six acres landscaped in the Gardenesque design and a conservatory filled with period flora personalize the landmark where visitors also enjoy concerts, lectures, workshops, festivals, teas and tours. Scarce Spanish Red Morgantown glassware (above) highlights Cauldon porcelain place settings and King's Pattern flatware at Christmas.

Man of a million lights, Rich Faucher (following pages) illuminates the holidays for 60,000 visitors from five states. "I discovered the real meaning of Christmas years ago," says the father of six who makes Boeing aircraft parts in Ridley Park, Pennsylvania. "And there really is a Santa Claus. I try to keep that spirit alive." With nearly 80,000 strings of lights, he creates a different display each year. "When one display ends," he says, "the next one starts. It's Christmas 365 days a year here." Faucher recently doubled his 200-amp electrical service to accommodate the one-acre light show on Santa Claus Lane near Red Lion. Called the Delaware Santa, he answers more than 1,000 letters, supports Toys for Tots, Make-A-Wish and Sunshine foundations and lights the Ronald McDonald House in Rockland. "Every now and then, I sneak down the chimney, but Santa really enters through the heart."

"I'm part of a team that develops new materials, processes and applications for holograms," says physical chemist Sylvia Stevenson (right), working in a laser lab at the DuPont Company's Experimental Station. "I usually tell the Girl Scouts when they visit a hologram is a lot like a photograph. Both record light but a hologram also records the distance light travels from an object. Our business, DuPont Holographic Materials, produces a photopolymer film for recording holograms." Commercial applications include three-dimensional images used as security devices. "But our bigger market," adds Stevenson, a Californian with an Iowa State University doctorate, "is components that go into flat panel displays for devices like LCD watches, cell phones, pagers and laptop computers." One of the first research laboratories in the country, the Experimental Station opened in 1903 north of Wilmington on the original site of the employee country club. About 5,000 people, including 1,000 Ph.D.s, work at the 129-acre site overlooking Brandywine Creek where nearly two centuries earlier French chemist Eleuthère Irénée duPont founded what was to become America's largest chemical and materials company.

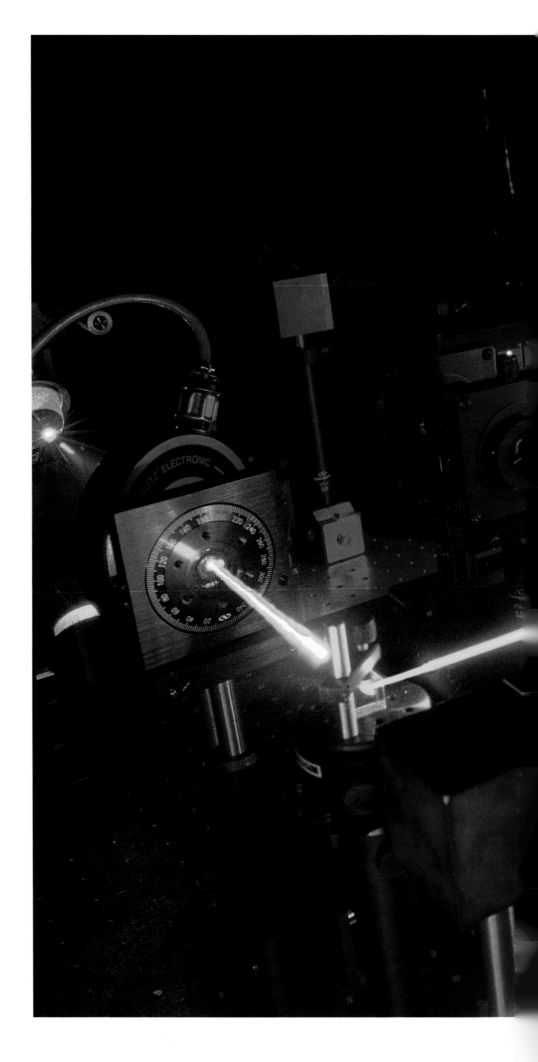

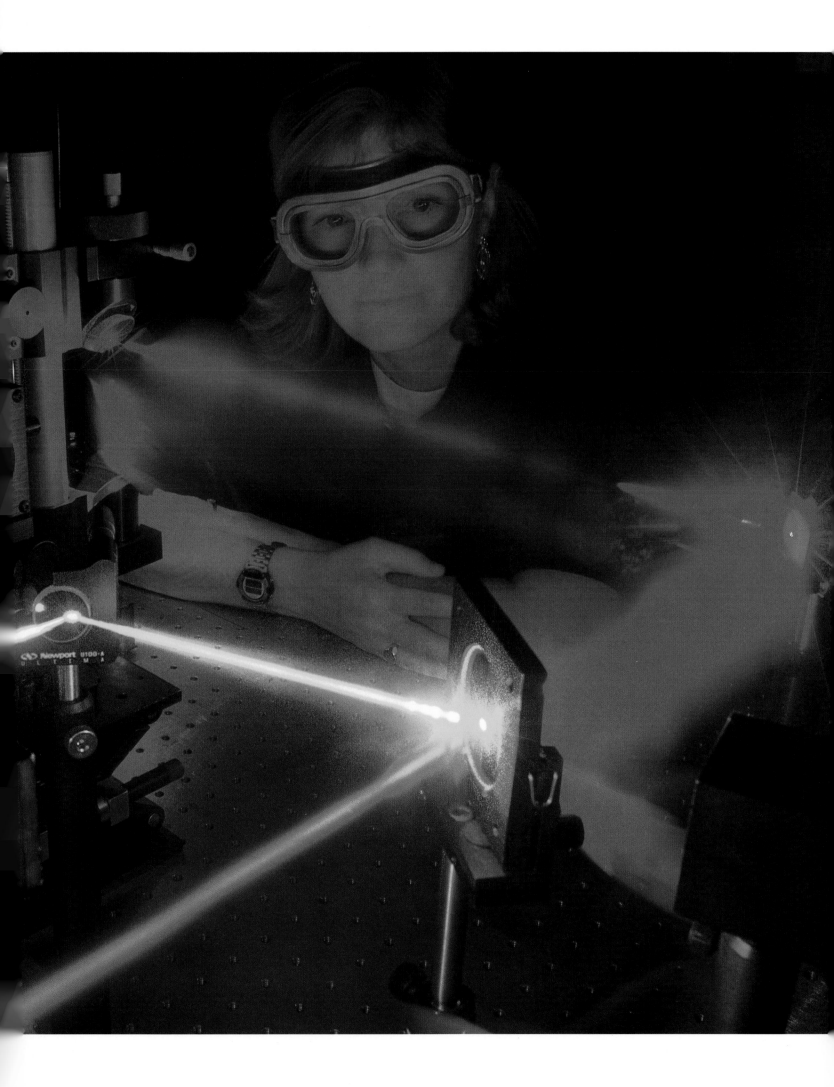

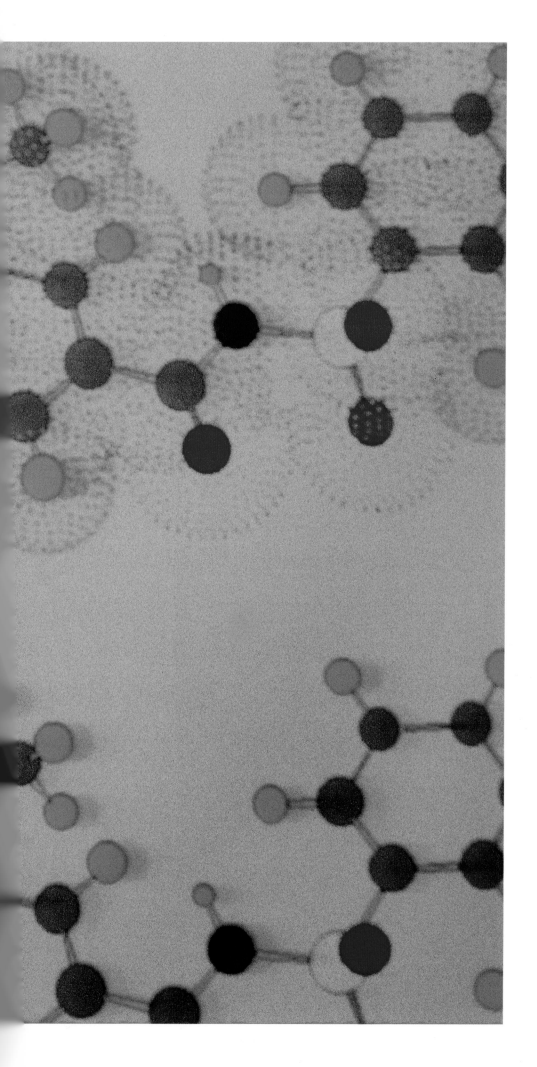

"You're looking at a schematic drawing of the molecule that is the active ingredient in a pill one can take for asthma," Dr. Fred Brown (left) says of Accolate, the prescription medicine he and his colleagues discovered about 12 years ago at Zeneca in Wilmington, long before his company's recent merger with Astra AB of Sweden. "We launched the drug in 1996 for U.S. consumption. People who were missing work and school because of asthma could go back to their normal lifestyle. Many asthma-sufferers have told us Accolate made all the difference in their lives."

The newly created AstraZeneca PLC, a $35 billion union of London-based Zeneca Group PLC and Astra, is one of the top five pharmaceutical companies in the world. Wooed by Delaware's $40-plus million tender of land and cash incentives, the pharmaceutical giant plans to locate its North American headquarters on 86 acres across from Zeneca's Fairfax campus. The coup landed New Castle County more than 2,000 jobs and millions in state tax revenues. Governor Tom Carper commented having both AstraZeneca and the DuPont Company on First State soil brings "international attention to Delaware as a cradle for biotechnology."

"We only march half the distance, but we have twice as much fun as the Mummers," says Jack Schreppler, self-appointed unofficial grand marshal-for-life of Middletown's Hummers Parade. An annual rite since the early 1970s, the town's spoof of Philadelphia's traditional New Year's Day march also roasts local and national personalities and events with impromptu costumes and floats (right). "The only rule is that taste doesn't count," Schreppler says of the hourlong Broad Street spectacle that draws about 200 participants and always plays well with locals. "The difference between the Mummers and the Hummers is before you get too cold or too bored, the Hummers are done. The parade's been resilient and I think it will go on as long as it retains its original sense of silliness and irreverence."

A solid gold tackle by Jeff Saunders of Middletown High School and Oliver Wilson of Cape Henlopen High School momentarily stops Reggie Melvin (left) of Concord High School during the 44th Blue-Gold All Star Football Game. Jonathan Thornton of Alexis I. duPont High School (above) celebrates Blue's 30-12 victory in the annual Delaware Foundation for Retarded Children kickoff at the University of Delaware in Newark. After the 1998 benefit, the foundation dispersed $67,000 to 11 Delaware organizations that provide housing, vocational training and artistic opportunities to children and adults with mental disabilities. "It's a great football game, but it's so much more. We educate high school communities about people with disabilities," says Suzanne L. Higdon, game chairperson. Seventy players from 43 schools statewide accept invitations to participate. "We're not just interested in the best players. We want kids who are good citizens. An important part of Blue-Gold is the Hand-in-Hand Program where we match students from each high school to children with mental retardation," she says. "This event is unique. It's the only game of its kind in the country."

Powerhouse on the playing field, the University of Delaware football
team (preceding pages) tackles another Atlantic 10 Conference
challenge on home turf in Newark. The Fightin' Blue Hens, named for
the state's Revolutionary War troops who fought as fiercely as
gamecocks, have five national championships under their helmets and
were runners-up three other times. Legendary coach Tubby
Raymond's 277 victories rank him 10th on the all-time collegiate
coaching win list.

Futures in hand, graduates exult at the university's 150th
commencement. John Shuren (above) of Whiting, New Jersey,
weathers granddaughter Christina Shuren's special day. "It was so hot
and I didn't have my hat but it was a wonderful ceremony, almost
enough to make me cry. I was so happy for her." New Ark College
opened in 1834 as a degree-granting institution after the General
Assembly established its perpetual charter. Renamed Delaware
College in 1843, doors closed 16 years later for financial reasons and
the impending Civil War. The college reopened in 1870 under the
federal Morrill Land Grant Act and state legislation in 1921 created
the University of Delaware. Today, more than 100,000 alumni live
in 76 countries.

Pitching America's favorite pastime fills New Castle County stadiums with support for the Wilmington Blue Rocks (above), minor league affiliate of the Kansas City Royals, and the nationally ranked University of Delaware Blue Hens (left). Baseball is the university's oldest sport. Since fielding its first team in 1882, players have competed in 11 NCAA Division 1 tournaments and the 1970 College World Series. American Baseball Coaches Hall of Famer Bob Hannah has shaped the program since 1964.

"This is our seventh season and we've made the playoffs six times. That's always a positive," says Blue Rocks spokesman Steve Lenox. Competing in the eight-team Carolina League, the Blue Rocks also savor a league-leading average attendance of 4,500 a game at Daniel S. Frawley Stadium. "Minor league baseball comes down to affordable family entertainment," Lenox says. "We've drawn more than 2 million fans in the past six years. The majority, win or lose, keep coming back for more."

Early arrivals, Canada geese flock to winter feeding grounds along southern New Castle County's coastal wetlands. "There are now two distinct populations of Canada geese in the Atlantic Flyway," says Tony Florio, retired Delaware wildlife manager. "The 'wild' population and the 'locals' or non-migratory geese that live on reservoirs, golf courses and at corporate headquarters with large lawns. They've become suburbanized to the point where, since they're not harvested, they're a real problem."

Crown jewel of the First State's first capital, the 1732 New Castle Court House (right) was the meeting place of the Colonial Assembly and Delaware's first General Assembly. The brick building remained the State House until 1777 when fears of attack by the British Navy prompted establishment of an inland capital in Dover. The cupola of the Court House is the center of the 12-mile arc separating Delaware from Pennsylvania. Colonial Immanuel Church on the Green, prominent with its 19th century tower and steeple, is a foundation of the Episcopal Church in Delaware. Founded as Fort Casimir by the Dutch in 1651, New Castle was the first major port on the Delaware River and home to Declaration of Independence signers George Read, George Ross Jr. and Thomas McKean.

"The sunrise was the perfect touch with the water right there and the Delaware Memorial Bridge in the background. It was awesome," Judy Kiger (preceding pages) says of the moment shared with John Prater on New Castle's Delaware Street wharf. Countless sunrises earlier, William Penn first stepped on New World soil near here. After the British conquest of the Dutch in 1664, the town was granted to Penn and named New Castle. "There's a lot more in Delaware than where I live," says Kiger of Elsonboro, New Jersey. "I've worked at restaurants in New Jersey but I seem to do better in Delaware. I commute daily and also come over to go to malls, movies and to eat. I think about moving."

Strolling the Delaware River offers a southern vantage from Battery Park in Old New Castle (following pages). Each summer, thousands descend on Delaware's Colonial capital to celebrate Separation Day, the anniversary of New Castle, Kent and Sussex counties' June 15, 1776 split from Great Britain and Pennsylvania. New Castle served as the government seat of the "Three Lower Counties" of Pennsylvania from 1704 until separating from England and Penn family proprietors.

"I always wanted to live some place that was someplace, a destination," recalls Thomas William Tear (left), a special events and display coordinator who frequently blades Battery Park's pastoral pier and two-mile trail along the Delaware River. "Time seems to have passed it by. It's not just the river and the sky, but the sounds of the earth. It all blends together and makes you feel so connected. I find it magical and calming and I finally realized I do live somewhere that is someplace. New Castle is special. It's my home and I wouldn't trade it for anything."

Winding south on scenic Route 9 through the Augustine Wildlife Area and past such place names as Stumps Corners and Taylor's Bridge, a jogger (following pages) laps two counties near Fleming's Landing. There, a 19th century iron bridge with a wooden plank roadbed over the Smyrna River once linked New Castle and Kent counties.

Fiddling on the Fourth, Beatrice Webb (following pages) relaxes at the 1886 Hockessin home of Bart Ruby and Eileen Tierney. "All our friends come by after the parade and we make margaritas and keep them happy," says Eileen, sporting her stars and stripes shirt. "I wear it once a year. The Fourth means a lot to me because I've adopted this country. I was naturalized in 1965 and come from County Mayo in Ireland where there are a lot of problems. I celebrate America because there's no orange or green here and no question about whose country it is." The couple's Old Lancaster Pike frame house, one of the area's oldest with original fish scale slate roof, clapboard siding and unique two-sided porch, is, according to Bart who bought it in 1991, "Hockessin's version of Victorian." Signatures of first owners William and Sarah B. Kent appear in the basement and backyard carriage house.

Karimah Graham of Girl Scout Troop 801 (above) stands at attention during Wilmington's 132nd Memorial Day Observance & Parade. Organized by volunteer representatives from area patriotic groups, the city's annual salute honors fallen veterans from all wars.

Laying flowers at the Soldiers and Sailors Monument on Delaware Avenue reminds 78-year-old World War II Army veteran Albert J. Radick (left) of departed servicemen. "They put their lives on the line for our country. Going to the Memorial Day service pays respect," says the chaplain of VFW Post 615 who served under General George Patton in Europe and fought the Battle of the Bulge in the 35th Infantry. "The American people seem lax on participation and involvement in the armed services today, like they don't want to be bothered. Some day, their sons and daughters will be called to protect our country. We'll never get rid of war."

"It's just the Fourth of July in Hockessin," Jo Ann Van Heest says of the mayhem on her slippery side yard (following pages). "It was so hot that day. The best part was all these kids cooling off and having fun."

"The Delaware Memorial Bridge Twin Span is the one thing people equate with the state of Delaware. It's a landmark for sure," Delaware River & Bay Authority spokesman Jim Salmon says of the steel link (preceding pages) between the First State and New Jersey. The bridges shuttle about 31 million vehicles across the Delaware River each year and tolls generate $45 million annually for the self-sustaining authority.

Boating past and present (right) converges on the nearby Christina River as Lesley McKnight of the Wilmington Rowing Club and dad Spencer Foster scull past Henry Hudson's re-created Half Moon, docked for a tall ships festival heralding riverfront development. Buoyed by a $70 million investment from the state, Wilmington's waterfront is flowing toward a regional destination. Planners predict a fully developed site on the city's south side could draw five million visitors yearly.

Toasting good health, couples socialize at a 1950s soda fountain at the 39th Wilmington Heart Ball. The April fete at Wilmington Country Club pumps big bucks into the American Heart Association's coffers. "It was wonderfully successful. We netted $120,000," says Peggy Zugehar who chaired the event with Sandy Macdonald. "All ages come. It's like a kick-off for spring festivities in Wilmington.

"She's a gorgeous ship and the only one of her type in the country, plus she's got a large volunteer organization to run her," says David W. Hiott, captain of the re-created tall ship Kalmar Nyckel (left). "She's a very good generic 200-tonne Dutch-built pinnace of 1625, not a reproduction because a reproduction means a copy and we had no drawings. But she's very faithful in her styling." The original ship, built in Holland in the 1620s and purchased by the Swedish cities of Kalmar and Jonköping for the Royal Swedish Navy, left that country in 1637. After extensive repairs in the Netherlands from a North Sea storm, the three-masted vessel set sail for the New World, arriving in the Delaware Bay in mid-March, 1638 after a 10-week crossing. Purchasing land from Native Americans along Minquas Kill, now the Christina River, settlers established the Colony of New Sweden, now Wilmington. The nonprofit Kalmar Nyckel Foundation was established in 1986 to financially support and oversee the $3.2 million re-created ship, launched before 20,000 well-wishers on September 28, 1997. As a living history museum, a training vessel and Delaware's seagoing ambassador, the Kalmar Nyckel offers dockside tours and plies the Atlantic Ocean from Long Island Sound to Norfolk, Virginia. "The crew is all-volunteer except for me and my engineer. I have a pool of 70 volunteers and a crew of 34 is optimum to get from here to there," Hiott says. "For dockside tours, we take about 60 at a time. It's a steady turnover. Usually, there's a line. People stay 10 minutes to two hours, depending on their interest. It's a busy boat."

"This class of rowers over four years was more successful than any other, male or female," coach Brad Bates says of his St. Andrew's School girls varsity eight team (preceding pages) led by stroke Meaghan Keeley of Clarksburg, West Virginia. Victorious in their 1997 maiden trip to crew's Super Bowl, the Women's Henley-On-Thames Regatta in England, Delaware's only secondary school crew team again reached the finals, losing to the British Junior National Champions. The Middletown boarding school's women rowers, six of whom competed together all four years, twice defeated the 40 best U.S. and Canadian schools at Philadelphia's Stotesbury Regatta. "It's an exciting sport that demands complete team unity. Everyone's on an equal playing field. No one rowed before they came here," says Bates. "My job is to show them technique, give my expectations and sit back and watch the magic."

Hoopes Reservoir (right) safeguards two billion gallons of water for the city of Wilmington and its New Castle County customers. Although spring-fed, most of the 30-day emergency water supply is diverted from Brandywine Creek. The 200-acre reservoir on property once owned by T. Coleman duPont, is 130 feet at its deepest point and was built by the Wilmington Water Department on Old Mill Stream, a small tributary of Red Clay Creek northwest of the city. Flooding the area forever submerged duPont's summer home. The four-year project was completed in 1933 at a cost of $2.2 million and is named for the late Edgar M. Hoopes, a water department chief engineer. Along its conifer and hardwood perimeter, posted signs forbid fishing, boating and swimming in the 50-degree water. "It's an extraordinary natural asset. You couldn't build this reservoir today for love or money," says former Delaware Development Office director Nathan Hayward III who lives nearby. "The fact the city was wise enough to prevent development along its shores is important. It was a far-sighted project."

Reflective of another era, a circa 1810 springhouse
on Barley Mill Road near Hockessin (preceding
pages) sits atop a groundwater source and once
provided cool storage for dairy products and other
perishables. The outbuilding, a common sight in
northern New Castle County, is preserved on the
private Red Clay Reservation. The Ashland
Covered Bridge, one of two remaining in Delaware
and named for the once-bustling 19th century mill
community nearby, and the Ashland Nature
Center are also reservation landmarks. "There'll be
no building on this land," promises Russell Hands,
the reservation's manager. "We're preserving the
land. We do a lot of tree planting here."

Rare beef, Belted Galloways (right) graze on
Bayard Sharp's Centreville farm. Intrigued by the
cow's unique look, Sharp bought his first Belties
more than a decade ago and works diligently to
improve his herd of about 50. Without the layer of
backfat characteristic of most beef animals, this
breed of Scottish lineage produces exceptionally
lean and flavorful meat.

"You can get more milk out of Holsteins than
other breeds and they're easier to work with," says
dairy farmer Joe Vari who tends 150 bovines east
of Odessa (following pages). "It all depends on the
weather and feed quality how much milk you get
from them. I have a rolling herd average of 23,000
pounds per cow a year." Vari's 15-hour days start
with the first of two milkings at 3:30 a.m. He also
grows field corn, alfalfa and rye on the 135-acre
farm he leases. "It's long hours but it's rewarding.
I could be working eight-hour days and making
more money somewhere else but I've farmed
pretty much all my life. I'm my own boss and I
like it." Dairy farmers are a dying breed in
Delaware. "Numbers are down considerably over
the past 20 years," says state Department of
Agriculture inspector G. Robert Moore. "Statewide,
there are about 95 dairies. New Castle County has
only about six. The decline has quite a bit to do
with development, low prices for milk, retirement
and no one to take over the farm."

An 1860s hay and feed barn near Taylor's Bridge marks another growing season as Larry Jones (left) hoes, flanked by family pets Beethoven and Mrs. Gray. "I live to be outside," says the gardener raised in Wilmington. "I was always looking for land and wanted to get out of the city. We found 13 acres and moved here about three years ago. My wife, Mary Lee, calls it 'Little Bit of Heaven.' Getting out in wide open spaces before they disappear is important to me," he adds. "There's peace and quiet here. It's a dream come true."

Brushed with a fall palette, artist Jamie Wyeth's farm (preceding pages) straddles Delaware and Pennsylvania where three generations of Wyeths have drawn inspiration from the area's fields, streams and rolling hills. Jamie, while hewing to the family trait of romantic realism and rural subjects, carved his own niche in the 1960s with portraits of President John F. Kennedy and the provocative leather-clad subject of "Draft Age." Born into the Brandywine school of painting through grandfather N.C. Wyeth, one of the nation's most prolific illustrators, and father Andrew Wyeth, one of America's favorite artists, Jamie tends toward N.C. in style and substance. The Delaware Art Museum in Wilmington and nearby Brandywine River Museum in Chadds Ford, Pennsylvania display many Wyeth works.

"We're doing something that's never happened before in the history of painting. My students call it 'Loperism' until somebody finds a sensible name for it," says Wilmington artist Ed Loper (right). "I am an abstract colorist. I paint realistic pictures but I paint them with colors and abstract spaces." Spanning more than six decades, his work is inspired by French impressionist Paul Cézanne. "He's the Father of Cubism and he was the instigator." Loper studied under the late Violette de Mazia at Pennsylvania's Barnes Foundation. "I started painting professionally when I was about 20, so I knew how to paint already. I went there to learn from her how to understand art. And I learned," says Loper, who teaches 55 students at his North Ogle Avenue studio. "Painting is not talent, it's a seeing process and you learn to see. I look at something and if I think it's worthwhile in terms of lines and spaces and color, then I paint it. It's that simple."

Shades of autumn paint a Centreville hillside (right) north of Wilmington as nature splashes seasonal artistry on a local canvas.

Agriculture consultant Stewart Ramsey Jr. chose fall's familiar face for his first corn maze (following pages). "I call it my Jack O'Lantern Maze. Cutting it in was difficult because we waited too long. The corn was too high," he says of the four-and-a-half-acre plot on Thompson's Bridge Road next to his popular Ramsey's Pumpkin Patch. "My large cash crop is pumpkins, 12 acres, all retail, and 50 acres of high quality horse hay. Everybody who went in my maze really liked it but it was a failure from an economic standpoint because we didn't have enough awareness. We're going to try again this year and we'll have more going on than paths through a cornfield."

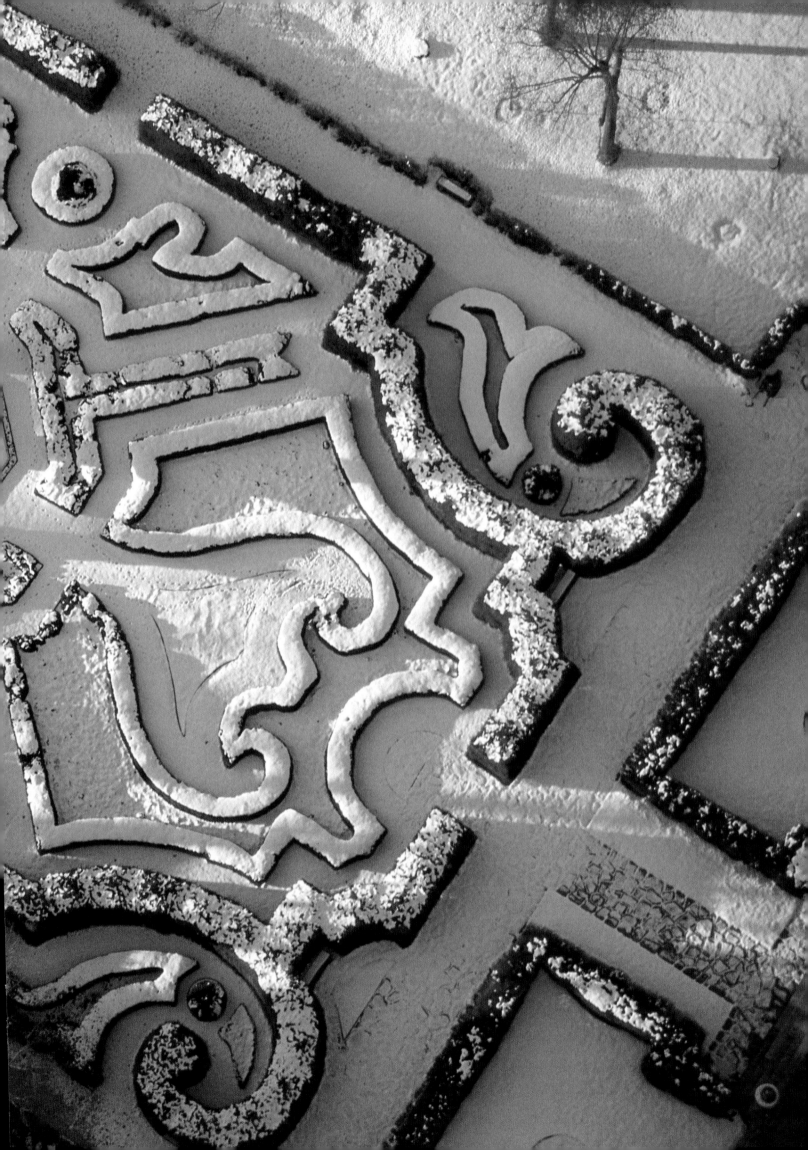

The Maze Garden at Nemours (preceding pages) complements an unparalleled vista at Alfred I. duPont's 300-acre country estate north of Wilmington. The maze, with hedges of Canadian hemlock and Hellert holly, is tilted for visibility from the 102-room mansion, a modified Louis XVI chateau of Brandywine granite quarried on site. Henri Crenier's 11-foot bronze statue, "Achievement," centers the plot. The grounds are among America's finest examples of French gardens. After the death of his wife, Jessie Ball duPont, in 1970, duPont's will stipulated his pink stucco residence be opened to the public. "We don't advertise. Nemours is quite different from any other tours in the area. We only take about 20 at a time in groups of six or seven and we give a very personalized tour," says mansion coordinator Paddy Dietz. Nemours is open by reservation May through November. duPont also founded the Alfred I. duPont Hospital for Children, a world-renowned facility, built in 1940 on the property.

Common throughout the state, the majestic great blue heron (left) and great white heron (following pages) find inviting habitat on Augustine Creek. The creek and its productive marshes provide feeding grounds for one of the nation's largest great blue heron nesting colonies. The upland heronry bears the name of conservationist J. Gordon Armstrong, who purchased the site in 1947. The creek and marshes were named centuries earlier by Augustine Herrman, holder of one of the original land grants and mediator of a dispute between William Penn and George Calvert. To the north and south of Augustine Beach is the Augustine Wildlife Area

Near New Castle, fall foliage (pages 146-147) accents the edge of the Delaware River, one of the East Coast's busiest shipping lanes.

Splendor in the grass, azaleas annually unfurl a traffic-stopping show on U.S. 13 northbound in Odessa (preceding pages) where Helen and Jerry Unruh tend 1,033 plants on little more than an acre. "People from all over stop and look but we don't do it for the public, we do it for ourselves," says Jerry, a World War II paratrooper and former state legislator who planted 80 bushes in 1952. "We picked the varieties so the whole yard explodes with color at the same time. Their peak period is about 10 days but we have them five weeks or more starting the first of April. I hate winter. Azaleas come along and kick winter in the tail end."

When Sara Whitworth (left) relocated to New Castle County in 1980, her real estate agent praised the Wilmington Flower Market as the perennial family-friendly fund-raiser for area charities. She dug in the following year selling tickets for children's rides and has been volunteering ever since. "It's just a wonderful, fun thing to do for a wonderful cause," says Whitworth, whisking flowers bought on break back to the Potpourri and Toys tent where she is basket coordinator with her sister, Martha Conaty. "In our particular tent, we've been involved for so many years, we're all good friends." A Wilmington tradition just before Mother's Day, the 78-year-old event is rooted in Rockford Park and raises about $200,000 over three days.

Spring blossoms under a lone tree (following pages) on Winterthur's nearly 1,000-acre property northwest of Wilmington.

On traffic surveillance, Corporal Christopher Dooner (preceding pages) of the Delaware State Police Aviation Section pilots a Bell 407 helicopter above the Delaware 1 bridge over the Chesapeake and Delaware Canal. The rotorcraft is one of four in the state police fleet manned by 10 pilots and 10 paramedics. "Our biggest impact," says Sergeant Jeff Evans, "is our EMS or emergency medical service to Delaware citizens and visitors. If they have a life-threatening injury, we are dispatched and they will be flown to a trauma center at no cost." "Our other big role is police work," says aviation commander Sergeant Dave Valeski. "Our helicopters are equipped with thermal imaging units and high intensity search-lights. We do searches of a criminal nature, surveillance and criminal photography and we can back up ground units. Police protection increases because we can cover a broader area in less time and see more."

Day's end filters through Wilmington, darkening the Delaware River to the east (right). The state's major urban center is home to a diverse population of about 73,000. Many still celebrate their ethnicity, a proud legacy from European forebears who settled the city in 1638 and later worked in Wilmington's factories, mills, railroad shops and shipyards. "I like to say Wilmington is a city of festivals," says director of cultural affairs Valerie Trammel. "We have Jazz, Tall Ships, Greek, Italian, Polish, Hispanic, African, Caribbean and Blues festivals. The variety really reflects the diversity of the city." A cultural cornucopia, Wilmington offers sublime sophistication at numerous venues rich in museums and historical sites.

Philadelphia photographer Jenna Kelley (following pages) shoots a twilight scene at Brandywine Creek State Park. "I look for good light, composition, design and aesthetically pleasing subjects," says the former Art Institute of Philadelphia student whose goal is owning her own studio. "For now," she says, "I'm just trying to get out there and see all I can see."

Eclipsed by a moonrise, nightfall descends on downtown Wilmington.

Portfolio Books
Post Office Box 156 • Rehoboth Beach, Delaware 19971

film processing by K.R.R.B., Newark, Delaware • color scans by Baltimore Color Plate, Towson, Maryland
photo and production assistance by Jenna Kelley • proofreading by Ken Mammarella and J.L. Miller

printed and bound in Hong Kong by Dai Nippon Printing Co., Ltd.